NLP

Thorsons First Directions

NLP

Joseph O'Connor & Ian McDermott

Thorsons
An Imprint of HarperCollinsPublishers
77–85 Fulham Palace Road
Hammersmith, London W6 8JB

The Thorsons website address is: www.thorsons.com

Published by Thorsons in 2001

10 9 8 7 6 5 4 3 2 1

Editor: Jo Kyle
Design: Wheelhouse Creative Ltd.
Production: Melanie Vandevelde
Photography: Photodisc Europe Ltd.

A catalogue record for this book is available from the British Library

ISBN 0 00711037 5

Printed and bound in Hong Kong

Contents

NLP

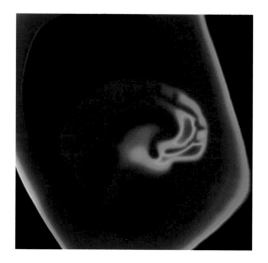

is neuro-linguistic programming: the

psychology of excellence

What is NLP?

Its title gives one answer. 'Neuro' refers to the mind and how we organize our mental life. 'Linguistic' is about language, how we use it and how it affects us. 'Programming' is about our sequences of repetitive behaviour and how we act with purpose. So NLP is about connection, for our thoughts, speech and actions are what connects us to others, the world and to the spiritual dimension.

This book explains how NLP translates into your everyday life. Although well grounded in psychological theory and research, NLP is first and foremost about action. It gives you more choices in your mind and body, and so frees you to explore your spirit.

The starting point of NLP is curiosity and fascination about people. It is the study of the structure of subjective experience. How do we do what we do? How do we think? How do we learn? How do we get angry? And how do outstanding people in any field get their results? To answer these questions NLP explores how we think and feel and studies or 'models' excellence in every walk of life. The answers can then be taught to others. The goal is excellence for all.

Origins of NLP

NLP began in the early 1970s when Richard Bandler, a student of psychology at the University of California, Santa Cruz, began working with John Grinder, then Assistant Professor of Linguistics. They developed a process, called 'modelling', by which they could discern the sequence of ideas and behaviour that enables a person to accomplish a particular task. Together they modelled three people: Fritz Perls, the innovative psychologist and originator of Gestalt therapy; Virginia Satir, the prime force behind family therapy; and Milton Erickson, a clinical hypnotherapist, whose ideas are continued in Ericksonian hypnotherapy. They also drew on the insights and ideas of many others, particularly Gregory Bateson, the British writer and thinker on anthropology, cybernetics and communications theory. Their first models dealt with verbal and non-verbal communication skills. Consequently, NLP has given rise to a trail of techniques that can be used both personally and professionally. They are used internationally in fields such as sports, business, sales and education, and enable us not only to reach out and influence others, but also to reach in and unify all the different parts of ourselves. You will learn how to aquire these skills, and more, in this book.

NLP is 'the psychology of excellence'.
It has a vision of a world in which
there is no shortage of excellence and
where education is about helping
everyone to be outstanding.

Presuppositions

This book is arranged around the basic
operating principles, or presuppositions,
of NLP. They are called presuppositions
because you presuppose them, that is,
you act as if they were true and notice the
results you get. They are actually working
hypotheses that may or may not be
literally true. NLP does not claim they are
true. The question to ask is not 'Are they
true?' but 'Are they useful?'

There is no orthodox list of NLP
presuppositions, so we have selected the
ones that are most commonly used and
which we think are the most important.

The Four Pillars of Wisdom

There are four main principles in NLP and we will be returning to them from different angles throughout this book.

The first and foremost principle, or pillar, is relationship, specifically, that relationship of mutual trust and responsiveness known as rapport. It can be applied both to your relationship with yourself and to your relationship with others.

We begin with the rapport you have with yourself. The greater the degree of physical rapport you have with yourself, the greater your health and well-being, for the different parts of your body are working well with each other. The greater your mental rapport with yourself, the more you feel at peace with yourself, for the different parts of your mind are united. Rapport at the spiritual level can manifest as a sense of belonging to a larger whole, beyond individual identity, and knowing our place in creation.

There are many who have all the external trappings of success, yet are unhappy within themselves. You may have noticed that such people make others uneasy too. We seem to arrange the world in a way that reflects our internal state. So internal conflicts create external

ones and the quality of the rapport we have with ourselves is often a mirror of what we achieve with others.

Whatever you do and whatever you want, being successful will involve relating to and influencing others. So the first pillar of NLP is to establish rapport with yourself and then others.

The second pillar is to know what you want. Without knowing what you want, you cannot even define what success is. In NLP this is known as setting your goal or outcome. It is a whole way of thinking. You consistently ask yourself, 'What do I want?' and others, 'What do you want?'

The third pillar is known as sensory acuity. This means using your senses: looking at, listening to and feeling what is actually happening to you. Only then will you know whether you are on course for your goal. You can use this feedback to adjust what you are doing if necessary.

The fourth pillar is behavioural flexibility. You have many choices of action. The more choices you have, the more chance of success. Keep changing what you do until you get what you want. This sounds simple, even obvious, yet how many times do we do just the opposite?

Logical levels

We build relationships on different levels. The American researcher and
NLP trainer Robert Dilts uses a series of what he calls neurological
levels that have been widely adopted in NLP thinking. They are very
useful for thinking about building rapport and personal change.

The first level is the environment (the where and when).
The environment is the place we are in and the people we are with.
You have probably heard people say that they were in the 'right place
at the right time'. They are attributing their success to their
environment. At this level, shared circumstances build rapport.

The second level is behaviour (the what).
This is the level of our specific, conscious actions: what we do. In NLP
behaviour includes thoughts as well as actions. What we do is not
random; our behaviour is designed to achieve a purpose, although this
may not always be clear, even to us. We may want to change our
behaviour, smoking or constantly losing our temper, for example. But
sometimes unwanted behaviour may be difficult to change because it
is closely connected with other neurological levels.

The third level is capability (the how).

This is the level of skill: behaviour that we have practised so often it has become consistent, automatic and often habitual. This includes thinking strategies and physical skills. We all have many basic intrinsic skills, such as walking and talking, and also consciously learnt skills, such as reading or playing a musical instrument.

The fourth level is beliefs and values (the why).

This is the level of what we believe is true and what is important to us. Beliefs and values direct our lives to a considerable extent, acting both as permissions and prohibitions. Are there some skills you would like to develop, but think you can't? As long as you believe you can't, you won't. We are also capable of holding conflicting beliefs and values, resulting in actions that contradict each other over time.

The fifth level is identity (the who).

Have you heard someone say something like 'I am just not that kind of person'? That is an identity statement. Identity is your sense of yourself, your core beliefs and values that define who you are and your mission in life. Your identity is very resilient, although you can build, develop and change it.

Finally, the sixth level is the spiritual level.
This is your connection to others and to that which is more than your identity, however you choose to think of it. Rapport at this level is described in spiritual literature as being one with humankind, the universe or God.

When NLP was developed in the early 1970s, there was a gap in psychological thinking. The Behaviourist psychology of the time was about action and reaction, stimulus–response, the interaction between environment and behaviour. There were also many value-based psychological systems, stressing beliefs, relationships and self-actualization. What was conspicuously missing was the how to – the capability level. NLP stepped into this gap by providing step-by-step procedures to make excellence easily learnable.

Changing levels

Knowing the logical levels is very useful in personal change and personal development work. Change is possible at any level. The question is, which will have the most leverage, that is, give the greatest result for the smallest effort? A change at the belief level is likely to affect skills and behaviour a great deal, a change in identity even more so. You can work from the top down or from the bottom up, all the levels relate together systemically.

Rapport

NLP uses the word rapport, as we have seen, to describe a relationship of trust and responsiveness. Rapport is essentially meeting individuals in their model of the world. We all have different upbringings, experiences and ways of

being. We are all unique, with different beliefs, capabilities and identities. We all see the world differently. To gain rapport with others you need to acknowledge them and their view of the world. You do not have to agree with it, just recognize and respect it. Rapport can be established (or broken) at many different levels.

Body language

We build rapport, and therefore trust, in a face-to-face meeting in many ways: with our words, our body language and our voice tone. The words are the most obvious part of any conversation, yet they are only the tip of the communication iceberg.

One of the keys to good relationships is acknowledging others and giving them the attention they deserve. One way excellent communicators do this is by matching body language with the person they are with. Adopt a similar posture. Give the same amount of eye contact. Match the speed and general frequency of hand gestures. Matching is not mimicry, however. Exact copying is not respectful. People quickly notice it and think you are mocking them. Mismatching is the opposite of matching. It is also a useful skill. Do you want a way to extricate yourself from a conversation without appearing rude? Mismatch body language. Looking away or increasing the rate of head nodding are some ways.

Voice

We can also establish rapport with others by matching their voice tone. We do this to some extent without thinking. When your companion is soft spoken, it is natural to moderate your own voice. Voice matching is not mimicry, more like two instruments harmonizing. The easiest way to experiment is to match the volume and the speed of the other person's voice.

Words

Words can also establish rapport. First, using the same technical vocabulary, where appropriate, is one way of establishing professional

credibility. Secondly, people will often mark out words and phrases that are important to them. Using the same words or phrases in your reply shows them you hear and respect their meaning.

Pacing and leading

Matching body language, voice tonality and words, and respecting beliefs and values are examples of what NLP calls pacing. Pacing is having the flexibility to meet others in their model of the world, rather than expecting them to fit in with yours. Pacing establishes a bridge. Once you have that, you can lead another person to other possibilities. You cannot lead without first pacing and gaining rapport.

Congruence

What would it mean to pace and lead yourself – to be in rapport with yourself? Rapport between mind and body is called congruence in NLP. Congruence means that your body language, tonality and words carry the same message. Your beliefs and values line up with your actions.

However, congruence is not perfection. It is not that all of you is playing exactly the same tune, but all the parts of you are at least following the same score.

Multiple descriptions

Central to NLP is an appreciation of the value of having different points of view of the same event. This is called having a multiple description. NLP distinguishes three main points of view: to be able to act wisely you need all three perspectives.

First position is your own reality. Think of a time when you were intensely aware of what you thought and believed, regardless of other people. You have just experienced being in first position, regardless of exactly what you thought about.

Second position is taking another person's point of view. You think, 'How would this appear to them?' Matching body language helps in taking second position. Because communication is an interactive process, the more you can understand how the other person is thinking and feeling, the better you can communicate to get what you both want from the interaction.

Third position is the ability to take a detached point of view and appreciate the relationship between you and the other, and to have a different relationship with yourself. This is an important skill.

That is Not What I Meant At All...

Rapport is the first step in good communication. Have you been in a situation where you said something you thought was clear, only to be amazed at the response? An innocent remark is taken personally or a well meant offer of help refused with a reply like 'Don't interfere!' The offer was clear to you but not to the listener. This can happen in reverse as well, when what you understood was not what the other person meant.

When we communicate, our goal is to transmit meaning. How do we know we have succeeded? When the other person gets that message. A sender cannot decide what the signal will actually mean to the other person, only what they would like it to mean. There is no such thing as failure in communication – you always succeed in communicating something. It just may not be what you intended to put across. The responses you get give you valuable pointers about what to do next. They are your teachers.

One NLP presupposition sums this up:

The meaning of the communication is the response you get.

What would be the consequences of acting as if this NLP presupposition is true?

You might get curious. How are misunderstandings possible? And how can they be prevented? This is usually done by paying attention to the other person's response, rather than by mind-reading or wishful thinking. Just by paying close attention you could pick up any misunderstandings before going miles out of your way and before they have serious consequences.

This is important in business, for example, where managers want to motivate rather than to antagonize their colleagues, and where miscommunication about prices and quantities of goods can result in large financial losses.

Exploring relationships

A relationship is two people eliciting responses from each other. If you want a change in response, then you must change your own actions. This will change the meaning for the other person and the spell is broken. Most of us have a relationship where we think, 'If only that person would stop acting that way, then everything would be fine.' It may be a family member or a work colleague. Think of a relationship like that to explore further.

What do you think it is about their behaviour that is the problem? For example, you may feel they are aggressive, insensitive or fault finding,

so you may feel browbeaten, angry or irritated. Label both your own and the other person's behaviour. You might wonder at which logical level you are threatened. Is this an identity issue for you? Or does it challenge your beliefs and values? Even thinking about this relationship can put you into an unresourceful state. You do not want to carry that into what you do next, so think of something different. Move, shake off that feeling. In NLP this is called changing state.

Secondly, imagine what the relationship is like from the other person's point of view. This is going to second position. How do they experience your behaviour? What sort of label would they put on it? How do they feel? Shake off that emotional state before continuing.

Now, go outside the relationship, become a detached observer. This is going to third position. A good way to do this is to imagine both of you on a stage. See how you respond to each other.

Shift your question from 'How can I change that person's behaviour?' to 'How am I reinforcing or triggering that person's behaviour?' How else could you respond? What prompts your behaviour?

When you communicate you are seeking to influence another person: you have an outcome in mind. Deciding what you want is the second pillar of NLP and the subject of the next chapter.

Deciding What You Want

Everything we do has a reason behind it. We always want something, although we are not always clear what it is. This applies right down to the most mundane levels. When you are hungry, your goal is to eat, when you are tired, your goal is to sleep. The streets are full of people, walking, driving, catching buses, trains and aeroplanes, and all of them are going somewhere for a reason.

So the presupposition of NLP is:

Human behaviour is purposeful.

What do you want? You have long-term and short-term goals, those things you want and need: possessions, skills, work, relationships, states of mind, ways of working or being. NLP calls these outcomes – results that you want to create in the world. An outcome is much more specific than a goal. You only have an outcome when you know what you will see, hear and feel when you have it. Goals are what you want. Outcomes are what you create. Setting outcomes is the key to becoming the dominant creative force in your life.

Outcomes

We fail to achieve our outcomes for three main reasons:
- they may not be realistically achievable
- they may be insufficiently motivating
- and, although they are desired, they may not be desirable from a wider viewpoint.

To turn a goal into an outcome, to make it realistic, achievable,

motivating and desirable, you have to explore it from different points of view.

• Make sure it is expressed in the positive.
This means moving towards what you want, not away from what you do not want. To turn a negative outcome into a positive, ask, 'What would this goal do for me if I got it?' or 'What do I want instead?'

• Determine what you have to do and what others have to do.
Have as much of the outcome under your direct control as possible. If others need to act for you, think how you can arrange a 'win–win outcome'. We can achieve little without others and unless you think out the consequences from their viewpoint so you both win, they may not help you again. Ask yourself, 'What do I need to do to ensure others want to help me achieve my outcome?'

• Make the outcome as specific as possible.
Imagine it in as much detail as you can. How long will it take? Set a realistic time limit, with an exact date if possible. Where and when do you want this goal? In which places, situations or parts of your life do you want it? With whom do you want the goal and with whom do you not want it? The more specific your outcome, the more real it becomes and the more you will notice opportunities to achieve it.

• Be clear about your evidence for achievement.
How will you know you have achieved your outcome? The evidence is through your five senses. What exactly will you see? What exactly will you hear? What exactly will you feel? What is the last piece of evidence before you get the outcome? For example, evidence for being more healthy might be that you will be the correct weight, with an improved complexion, and others will notice the difference.

You cannot achieve an outcome, or learn anything, without feedback and the sooner the feedback comes the better. The longer the time between action and feedback, the harder it is to learn and adjust.

• Consider the resources available to achieve this outcome.
Obvious resources are money and material possessions that you can use directly. People are resources. They may be able to help you directly or as role models. You can also use historical or fictional characters as role models. Personal qualities and skills are also resources. If you need certain qualities, think about how you could develop them.

• Consider the consequences of achieving your outcome.
Think of your outcome from different points of view. One of the best ways to explore the consequences is to take second position with significant other people. How does your outcome appear from their point of view? How does it affect them? How do they feel about it? When you think like this you will gain trust and help.

What else would happen? What will you have to give up by getting what you want? Also think about the time, money and the effort, both mental and physical, you will need to invest. Is the goal worth it?

• Recognize the positive by-products of your present behaviour.

Invariably the present situation will have some good qualities. How can you incorporate them into your outcome, so that you keep what is good about your present circumstances?

• How does your outcome relate to your larger plans?
Your outcome is likely to be part of a larger outcome. Relate it to your other plans and outcomes. What does it help to achieve and why is this important?

   When you connect your outcome to your values and life plans, it will be motivating. It is difficult to commit to an outcome that seems unimportant and disconnected from the rest of your life.

• What smaller outcomes may be part of this outcome?
Your outcome may be large and unwieldy as it stands. There may be obstacles. You may need to break it down into a series of smaller, more manageable outcomes. Decide on the right sequence in which to do them, then begin.

• Lastly, does this outcome feel right to you?
Is it congruent with your sense of self, your identity? Is it you? If it is, take your insights and form an action plan, including one thing you can do immediately. Unless you act, the outcome will remain a dream.

Getting in a State

A state is your way of being at any moment; the sum of your thoughts, feelings, emotions, mental and physical energy. States vary in intensity, length and familiarity. Some have names, for example, love, fascination, alertness, anger, jealousy, fatigue or excitement, while others are less easy to pin down – we may feel in a 'good mood' or a 'bad mood' or just 'out of sorts'. The state you are in is very important. It affects your health, the quality of your decisions and how successfully you carry out a task.

Everyone knows we respond to outside events, becoming angry, excited, loving or exasperated in response to other people and situations. But not so many realize that we can change our state at will. This has far-reaching implications for how we affect others and how successful we are in the world.

The next two NLP principles go together:

> **Having choice is better than not having choice.**

> **People make the best choice they can at the time.**

When you have choice about your state, you have more emotional freedom. The choices people make are limited by the states they find themselves in. When we increase the range of choice – and so increase our emotional freedom – we will have more, perhaps better, choices.

Becoming aware

If you want to change your present state, the first thing is to become aware of it, for you cannot deliberately change a state you are unaware of.

Start from where you are. Explore the state you are in at the moment. Give it a name. Be aware of your body. Notice the feelings you have in the different parts of your body. If you are uncomfortable, change position. Now be aware of any mental pictures you might have. Do not try to change them. Become aware of any internal voices or sounds. How much mental and physical space do you have? Get a sense of your boundaries. Now you have turned the spotlight of consciousness on your state, notice how it has changed.

Your baseline state

Some states you 'visit' more than others and there are a small number that you return to regularly. Of these, one will be your baseline state, that familiar state where you feel most at home. Is your home a comfortable and well-furnished one? If it had a name, what would it be? Is your baseline state balanced and harmonious or do you habitually feel unbalanced and incongruent? What do you like about it and what would you add if you could?

   When your baseline state is long established, it can seem the only way to be, instead of only one way to be. If you are uncomfortable in your baseline state, remember you can change it like any other and custom design one that is a pleasure to return to.

Anchors

The two most important questions so far are, 'What state do I want to be in to make best use of what is happening to me?' and then, 'How can I arrange it?'

Our states are constantly changing as we react to the environment. To have choice about your state, you need to know what triggers it.

The sight and sound of certain things will change your state. NLP calls any stimulus that changes our state an anchor. An anchor may be visual, like the sight of a newborn baby or holiday photographs. It may be auditory, like an advertising jingle, or kinesthetic, like a handshake or a relaxing massage. It may be olfactory, like the smell of roses, or gustatory – a particular taste that evokes a

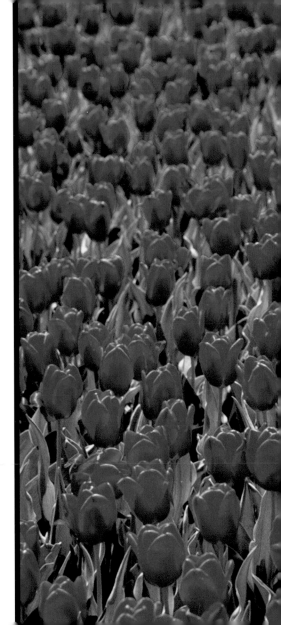

specific feeling or memory. It may be external, in the environment, or internal, within the mind, and it can operate at every logical level – for example, your name is an anchor for your identity, and religious symbols are anchors for beliefs and values.

Some anchors are almost universal. What makes them universal is our human ability to link stimulus to response without thinking, so you do not have to evaluate every stimulus you receive. Do you evaluate a red traffic light every time you see one?

We consciously choose very few of our anchors, they have been built up randomly throughout our lives. Many of them are neutral and some trigger unresourceful states. Many anchors are linked to the past and may be out-of-date.

The first practical step is to become aware of the anchors that put you in an unresourceful state. Once you know them, you can choose whether or not to respond.

The second step is to design your own anchors.

Using anchors to change state

Using anchors is the key to designing, changing and choosing your baseline state, or any other state you wish. Choose the resources you want, associate them to an anchor, and then consistently use that anchor to bring those resources into the present moment.

The NLP presupposition is:

> We either already have all the resources we
> need or we can create them.

What is difficult sometimes is bringing them to where they are needed. There are three ways to access resources.

• Find a role model.
You may have got your baseline state from a role model without realizing. Now you can pick one that appeals to you. It can be a real or fictional character. 'Try on' that character for size. What would it be like to be that character? What sort of state allows them to act as they do? What could you take that is valuable for you?

• Use your physiology.
This is the physical approach to states. Changing your physiology is the most direct way of changing your state. A stuck state, will show in stuck physiology; getting up and moving is the simplest action to change state. Smiling broadly, looking up and standing straight will change your state. Acting as if you feel good can start to produce those very feelings.

• Change your thinking.

One way to do this is to 'think of a time when...' For example, think of an experience you want to remember and enjoy. Go back into that scene, making sure you are 'associated' in the memory, i.e. seeing through your own eyes. Hear the sounds and voices and enjoy the good feelings again. On returning to the present you will have changed state.

Building a state with anchors

Here is a process that will build a resource state. First you have to decide what state you want. What resources do you want? You might need to face a challenge with humour, patience or curiosity.

Remember a time when you had that state and get back to it – see what you saw, hear what you heard and get the feeling as strongly as you can. If necessary, think of a role model and imagine living an episode as them in the state you want. Now, change state by coming back to the present.

Decide what associations or anchors you want to trigger that state. Pick one thing you can see in your mind's eye (a visual anchor), one sound or word you can say to yourself (an auditory anchor) and one small inconspicuous gesture you can make (a kinesthetic anchor). Some people use a clenched fist or touch two fingers together.

Go back and fully experience that resourceful state. Just before the resourceful feeling reaches its peak, see the picture, hear the sound and make the gesture. Then change your physiology, change state and think of something else.

Test your anchors. See the picture, hear the sound and make the gesture and notice how this brings back the resourceful feeling. If you are not satisfied, do it again. Do this as many times as you need, until the anchors bring back the resourceful feeling.

You have now set up your own anchors so that whenever you see that picture, hear that sound and make that gesture, it puts you into the state you want. You do not need all three anchors; indeed, some people use only one anchor. Find out what works best for you.

Once you have the ability to choose and change your states, your life will be different. You will not be a victim, you will have moved the locus of control from outside to inside yourself.

Reality Leaves a Lot to the Imagination

Human beings share the same five senses and the same basic neurology, yet see, hear and feel the world very differently. How do we make personal meaning from the events that befall us? First, we are not passive receivers of input, like a computer keyboard. We are active explorers of reality. Perception comes from the inside out. Every single brain is unique, and as we search out what interests and is important to us, we strengthen certain neural connections in our brains and weaken others. We are drawn to those things that interest us.

Our senses are the channels through which we perceive the outside world. Aldous Huxley called them the 'doors of perception' – sight, hearing, feeling, taste and smell.

The NLP presupposition is:

We process all information through our senses.

Our senses are receptive to certain aspects of whatever is out there. However, being conscious, we have the ability to decide which signals from the environment are the most important at a particular time and should come into our awareness over all the possible signals. We do not throw our doors of perception wide open or we would be totally overwhelmed. We have gatekeepers that we set on the doors: beliefs, values, interests, occupations and preoccupations all patrol the threshold to preserve us from sensory overload.

Our map of reality

What we finally perceive is a map of reality. Some parts are full of detail, others are sketchy and some may be completely empty. Having made our map, is it a good one? Is it well sign-posted and does it make it easy or difficult to get what we want?

One of the most important NLP presuppositions is:

> **People respond to their map of reality and not to reality itself.**

NLP is the art of changing our map for one that gives us more choice.

Representational systems

You make your map and you have to live in it. Remember two things as you create it:

1. How you use your senses on the outside is going to affect your thinking and experience on the inside.
2. You can change your experience by changing how you use your senses on the inside.

We have an incredible ability to create experience on the inside. A painful memory will make us wince again. A pleasant memory will make us smile and re-experience the pleasure. We represent our experience to ourselves using our senses, so in NLP the senses are called representational systems.

There are five representational systems:

Sight	(Visual, abbreviated to V)
Hearing	(Auditory, abbreviated to A)
Feeling	(Kinesthetic, abbreviated to K)
Tasting	(Gustatory, abbreviated to G)
Smell	(Olfactory, abbreviated to O)

From moment to moment we create our internal world using our representational systems. Once you know you create your internal world, you can start to create it the way you want it, rather than the way your brain does by default. Just as we develop skills and preferences in using our senses on the outside, so we do the same with our representational systems on the inside. What are your preferences? With a visual preference you may be interested in drawing, interior design and fashion, the visual arts, films,

mathematics and physics. With an auditory preference you may be interested in language, writing, drama, music, training and lecturing. A kinesthetic preference might be manifested in sport, carpentry, gymnastics and athletics. The more you use your senses on the outside and the more acute they are, the more you may favour them as representational systems. This does not mean you are typecast, only that you have certain strengths – and perhaps certain weaknesses if you tend not to use a particular representational system.

Know your preferences. Know your strengths and potentials. Many people think they have no talent for music, art or mathematics, when in fact they are just not using the best representational system for the task. Music involves the ability to hear internal sounds, while art and design need the visual system. Academic learning needs the ability to access a lot of information at once and to do this you need to use the visual system. As people are taught to develop their representational systems, they become naturally talented in ways they had not been before.

The physiology of thinking

How we think shows in our physiology. Here is the NLP presupposition that has been implicit in much of what we have discussed:

The mind and body are one system.

Visual thinking

People who are visualizing will tend to be looking up or level and their neck muscles are likely to be contracted. They may also furrow their brow as if trying to focus on something. (They are.) People who spend a lot of time visualizing may complain of headaches or a stiff neck. Breathing is a critical part of physiology. When visualizing, people tend to stand or sit erect and breathe high in the chest. Breathing like this results in shorter, more shallow breaths, so people who are visualizing will tend to breathe and speak more quickly.

Auditory thinking

Auditory thinkers tend to make small rhythmic movements of the body, often swaying from side to side. The voice tonality will be clear, expressive, often musical. Do you know anyone who habitually puts

their head on one side when they think? Some people will lean their head on their hand as if speaking on the telephone. They are listening to voices and sounds inside their head. You may also see their lips move as they form the words they are saying to themselves.

Kinesthetic thinking

Kinesthetic thinking is thinking with the body and will usually involve a rounded, even slumped posture. When people think this way, they will often look downwards, for this helps to get in touch with bodily feelings. They will tend to breathe abdominally, low in the body, and the voice is often lower and slower, because abdominal breathing is fuller and slower.

We do not suggest that there is such a thing as a universal body language. We all use all the representational systems and very many people will habitually favour one system. This being so, their physiology may take on some of these characteristics.

Representation system physiology

	Visual	Auditory	Kinesthetic
Posture	head up erect	often swaying, rounded, head to one side (telephone position)	head down
Breathing	high in chest	mid range	low in abdomen
Voice & Tonality	fast voice, higher pitched	melodic rhythmic	lower & softer
Eye Movements	up or defocus	midline or down left	down or down right

Eye accessing cues

NLP suggests that there is a link between the way our eyes move and the way we think.

Eye movements are known as eye accessing cues in NLP literature, because they enable us to access certain information. They cue us.

Eye accessing cues (NB This is as you look at another person.)

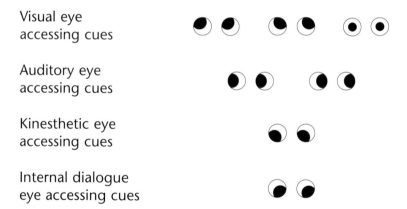

Visual eye accessing cues

Auditory eye accessing cues

Kinesthetic eye accessing cues

Internal dialogue eye accessing cues

Particular eye movements are linked to particular representational systems. In general, people will look upwards or defocus when they visualize. They will move their eyes sideways to the left or right when hearing sounds internally and they may look down to their right when thinking kinesthetically. Looking down to their left usually signifies internal dialogue. These movements are consistent and mostly unconscious. They are the general patterns, so do not take these as true for everyone all the time.

What are the practical applications of eye accessing cues? You can use them not only to find out how others are thinking but also to make it easier for yourself to think in particular ways: you are literally tuning in your body and mind, like tuning into a television programme. When you need to visualize, look up. When you need to contact your feelings, look down. Use accessing cues to help you think more precisely and clearly in the way you want to.

Speaking your mind

Language is rich and flexible and there are many different ways to express our thoughts. People often express the same idea differently using language from different representational systems. For example, we have friends who say, 'Be seeing you' (visual). Some say, 'I'll be hearing from you' (auditory). Others say, 'I'll be in touch' (kinesthetic).

NLP understands language as a reflection of inner experience. It is a surprisingly accurate translation of the way we think. The words and phrases that show which internal sense we are using are called predicates and predicate phrases in NLP.

Here are some common predicates to show you how they sound, so you can get a feel for the idea:

Visual Words and Phrases
Look, focus, imagination, see, watch, colour, dim, notice, illustrate, reveal, insight, blank, perspective.

I see what you mean.
Something to look
forward to.
It colours his view of life.
A dark cloud on the horizon.
The future looks bright.
Taking a dim view.
My point of view.

Auditory Words and Phrases
Say, loud, deaf, remark, discuss, speechless, silence, listen, music, harmony.

On the same wavelength.
Turn a deaf ear.
Speak your mind.
Word for word.
Loud and clear.
What do you say?

Kinesthetic Words and Phrases

(including taste and smell)
Touch, solid, warm, cold, rough, grasp, hold, gentle, heavy, weak, hot, smooth, move.

Get to grips with the idea.
Hold on a moment.
A cool customer.
Put your finger on it.
Heated argument.
A smooth operator.

Olfactory Words and Phrases

Nose, smell, pungent, fragrant.

Smell a rat.
Smelling of roses.
A nose for business.

Gustatory Words and Phrases

Spicy, sweet, bitter, salty.

A bitter experience.
A taste for the good life.
Saccharine sweet.

Know yourself and pace others

Sensory-based language is a powerful tool in communicating and influencing. First, know yourself. Find out your own language and thinking preferences. You can do this by writing or speaking into a tape recorder for a few minutes about your personal and professional life. Don't think about it, just write or say whatever comes into your head. Then notice what language predominates – seeing, hearing or feeling.

Start to notice how others express their thoughts. A person will consistently use language from their preferred representational system, so listening to them is the easiest way to find out which one they favour. Listen past the content of what a person says to how they say it. Once you have developed an ear for sensory language you will be able to pace others with language. Use words from the same representation system as they do. This will give you rapport on the verbal level. For example, someone says, 'I can't tell if this is right for me.' You reply, 'What more do you need to hear?' If they were to talk instead about getting a clear vision and then moving forward, you would pace them by talking in terms of seeing the way forward.

Thought connects with physiology and both connect with language. The next chapter will further explore how our maps of reality are translated into the skills we have and words we speak.

Customizing your Brain

Submodalities

The five representational systems – seeing, feeling, hearing, tasting and smelling – are the building blocks of our internal experience and are sometimes known as modalities.

Any distinction we can make with our senses in the outside world, we can also make in our inner world. For example, we see colours and sense distance in our mental world as well as in the outside world. In NLP these distinctions are called submodalities. Submodalities are the smaller building blocks of the senses, the way complete pictures, sounds and feelings are composed. They are the qualities that make each experience distinct.

An exercise

Make yourself comfortable and remember a pleasant memory. Look at your mental picture of it. If you find it hard to visualize, see whatever you can. Is the picture black and white or is it in colour? Is it moving or still? How bright is it? Are you looking at the scene through your own eyes or are you seeing yourself in the picture? These are all examples of visual submodalities. Let the picture fade.

Now listen to any sounds and voices in your memory. Are they loud or soft, near or far? Are they continuous? Are they clear or muffled? From which direction do they come? These are auditory submodalities. Let the sounds fade.

Now the feelings. Whereabouts in your body are they located? Is each feeling large or small? Warm or cool? How intense is it? How large is the area it covers? These are kinesthetic submodalities. Let these feelings fade. What is left?

Our memories, hopes and beliefs all have a submodality structure, and this is how we give them meaning. Then we have feelings about them. This is true whether they are unique events, for example, 'my first date', or classes of experience, for example, 'love', 'beliefs', 'confusion' or 'hobbies'.

Some of the most common submodality distinctions are listed on the following pages. There may also be others that are important to you.

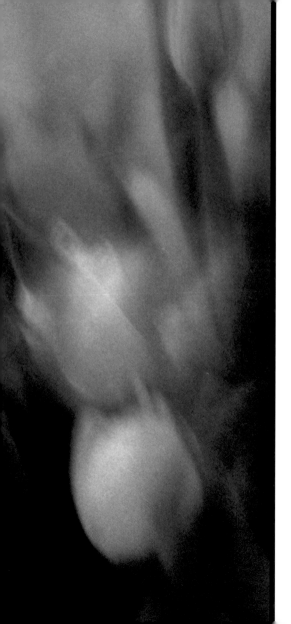

Visual Submodalities

associated (seen through own
   eyes) or dissociated
   (looking at self)
colour or black and white
framed or unbounded
depth (two- or three-
   dimensional)
location (e.g. to left or right,
   up or down)
distance of self from picture
brightness
contrast
clarity (blurred or focused)
movement (like a film or a
   slide show)
speed (faster or slower
   than usual)
number (split screen or
   multiple images)
size

Auditory Submodalities

stereo or mono

words or sounds

volume (loud or soft)

tone (soft or harsh)

timbre (fullness of sound)

location of sound

distance from sound source

duration

continuous or
  discontinuous

speed (faster or slower
  than usual)

clarity (clear or muffled)

Kinesthetic Submodalities

location

intensity

pressure (hard or soft)

extent (how big)

texture (rough or smooth)

weight (light or heavy)

temperature

duration (how long it lasts)

shape

Using submodalities

Submodalities offer tremendous opportunities for gaining control of our subjective experience because we can change them at any time. Take, for example, your experience of a negative state, say, boredom. How is it possible to experience boredom? Whatever the outside cause, the state itself will have a submodality structure. For example, when people describe being bored, they will typically talk about everything being 'flat' or 'grey'. They will use a typical tone of voice.

To change a state of boredom, determine its submodality structure in all representational systems. Then think of a state you would rather be in, for example, curiosity. Think of something you are very curious about and again determine the submodality structure of that state. Now take a step back and look at both sets of submodalities. How are they different? Go back to the bored experience (if you still can) and change the submodalities of boredom to those of curiosity. Notice how your experience is different.

When you are in a bored state, you cannot 'make' yourself curious by will-power, however much you may want to be. But changing submodalities gives you the practical means to change your state.

When we change the structure of the experience by changing the submodalities, then the meaning will also change. When the meaning changes, our internal response will also change.

Associated and dissociated states

Association and dissociation are two very important submodalities. You are associated when you are inside an experience, seeing through your own eyes. You are dissociated from an experience when you are outside it, seeing yourself at one remove.

   An associated experience is very different from a dissociated experience. When you are associated, you are in the experience and you get the bodily feelings, good or bad, 'associated' with the experience. Store pleasant memories as associated pictures to enjoy them again. When you are dissociated, you are outside the experience and do not experience the accompanying feelings. You might have wondered how it is possible for some people to look back on important and intense experiences and say they feel nothing. They do it by dissociating. Dissociating can be very useful; it keeps the feelings from painful memories at bay. It also enables you to learn from experience.

Modelling

In NLP, modelling means finding out how someone does something. It is the core of NLP, the process of replicating excellence. Modelling a skill means finding out how the person who has the skill thinks about it, and the beliefs and values that enable them to do it. You can also model emotions, experiences, behaviour, beliefs and values. NLP models what is possible. It is possible because human beings have already done it.

The NLP presupposition is:

Modelling successful performance leads to excellence. If one person can do something it is possible to model it and teach it to others.

To model a skill you focus on three neurological levels: what the model does (their behaviour and physiology), how they do it (the way they think) and why they do it (beliefs and values). You will also need to take into account the environment and the identity of the model.

To model a skill you need:
- the model's behaviour and physiology
- the way they think
- their beliefs and values.

NLP modelling has three main phases. The first phase is observing, questioning and being with the model when they are actually engaged in the skill you are interested in. You take second position with the model, becoming them as far as you are able. Direct questioning on its own can be disappointing, for a person who is very skilful has usually forgotten the learning stages and is unaware of exactly how they do the task. The work of the NLP modeller is to go beyond this barrier of consciousness and learn about the unconscious competence of the model.

When you have finished the first phase you will have a lot of information, and you will not yet be sure what is important and what is not. Some elements may be the personal style of the model. So the second phase is systematically to take out each facet of the model's behaviour to find out whether it makes a difference to the results you get. If it does, then it is an essential part of the model. If it does not, then it can be relinquished.

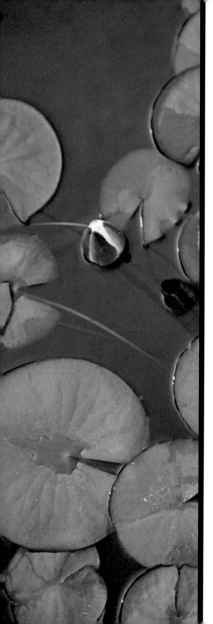

The third and final phase is to analyse what you have learned so that you can teach it to others.

There is an alternative way of modelling, which works better for some skills. Here you break down the task into small pieces and systematically set about acquiring them one by one until you have built the whole skill.

Once you have the skills of modelling, you can use them to model whatever interests you.

Mental strategies

Finding out how a person thinks – their mental strategies – is an important part of modelling. Mental strategies are how you organize your thoughts and actions to accomplish a task – from something simple, such as remembering a name, to something very complex, such as planning a career or falling in love. Just as large goals decompose into smaller tasks, complex strategies contain a number of smaller ones, like a series of Chinese boxes one inside another.

To model a strategy you need to discover:
- the representation systems used
- the submodalities of the inner pictures, sounds and feelings
- the sequence of steps.

Motivation strategies

Have you ever wondered how you motivate yourself to do something? Your motivation strategy will determine how easily you can get down and do a task. For example, one person we modelled looks first at the work she needs to do and hears a loud, encouraging, internal voice saying, 'Time to do this.' Then she constructs a big, bright, shiny mental picture of the finished work. Feeling good as she looks at that picture, she starts the work. This strategy works well and it pleasant to run. It moves towards a positive purpose.

This brings us to another NLP presupposition:

People work perfectly.

No one is wrong or broken. It is a matter or finding out how they function so that this can effectively by changed to something giving more useful or desirable results.

The Gatekeepers at the Doors of Perception

How do we create our model of the world from our experience? NLP suggests there are three gatekeepers at the doors of perception.

• The first is Deletion.
We are selective about our experience and leave parts out – we delete them. Either they do not register or we discount them as unimportant.

• The second is Distortion.
We change our experience, amplifying or diminishing it, and seeing it differently, as if in a fairground hall of mirrors.

• The third is Generalization.

We take certain aspects of our experience as representative of a whole class and pay no attention to exceptions. This is useful because it lets us respond to new situations on the basis of what we have learned from similar ones in the past. It is a problem if we generalize wrongly or do not stay open to new experience. Beliefs are examples of generalizations.

These gatekeepers are neither good nor bad in themselves; they are both an asset and a liability.

If we did not delete some sensory information we would be overwhelmed. However, we may be deleting just what we need to pay attention to, for example, how we are feeling or important feedback from others.

In the same way, if we did not distort we would stifle our creativity. When you are planning to redecorate, it is useful to be able to imagine

what a room is going to look like when it is finished. This is sensory distortion. But if you decide that when someone looks at you in a certain way they are really despising you, you run the risk of distorting the meaning of their look and then distorting your response.

When you generalize you aim to make sense of the world and know what to expect. This means that when you encounter a door handle that is differently shaped from any you have seen before, you do not have to retire puzzled. You know that it is just another kind of handle.

So generalization is a basic part of how we learn. But the same process can spell disaster. Suppose you had a difficult relationship and decided on the basis of that experience that all men or all women are the same – not to be trusted. Your generalization could stop you seeking out men and women who are exceptions to your rule.
So, through deleting, distorting and generalizing we can create a friendly or a hostile world. And the more we practise, the better we will get at making the world fit our filters.

People have biases on how they shape their perceptions. Some people will do more deleting, while others tend to distort more and yet others will be more given to generalization.

Language

NLP suggests these three gatekeepers transform sensory experience into internal representations. They also transform our internal representations when we use language. First we delete, distort and generalize our experience. Then our choice of words to describe the experience deletes, distorts and generalizes it all over again. Spoken language, then, is a map of a map and two levels away from sensory experience.

The world does not come with labels attached. We attach them and then forget we did so. We can mistake the words we attach to our experience for the experience itself and allow them to direct our actions.

We can use language in three ways to find out about and influence experience.

Firstly, we can ask questions that connect language with thought and back to sensory experience. For example, someone says to you, 'The people here are unfriendly.' This is a generalization, and we can ask a specific question like, 'Do you mean everybody? Is there no one at all here who is friendly?' This will make the person look at their generalization and see what basis it has in their experience. They will have to look at specific instances. This is called chunking down in NLP, going from a general case to more specific ones.

The second way we can use language is to go from specific instances to more general ones. We can use very permissive and vague language that allows the other person to find just that particular meaning that is right for them. This is called chunking up, going from a particular case to a general one.

Finally we can use language to chunk sideways: to compare one experience with another. This is the realm of metaphor, simile and story-telling, where you explain, allude or illuminate by comparison. This chapter heading is an example.

Language, Trance and Stories

As we have seen, language is very powerful, you cannot not respond to it. When we hear something we have to make some meaning out of it, so we search unconsciously for the way it could be relevant to us. The vaguer it is, the more possible meanings it has.

The Milton Model

NLP has studied this vague type of language and produced the Milton Model. The Milton Model is a way of constructing sentences that are rife with deletions, distortions and generalizations. It originated from the modelling work done by Richard Bandler and John Grinder on Milton Erickson's artfully vague use of language.

Milton Erickson was one of the foremost hypnotherapists this century. A client goes to a therapist because they cannot solve their problem consciously on their own. The resources they need are unconscious. Erickson used language to pace and lead the person's reality. He described their ongoing sensory experience in very general terms and then led them deeper into their own internal reality. He used complex language to distract their conscious mind and allow access to the unconscious resources. When the client was in a trance, Erickson

enabled them to search for the resources they needed from their unconscious with vague, open, permissive language and metaphors.

Trance

So the Milton Model originated in hypnotherapy and was used to induce trance. Trance is not a special state evoked only by skilled hypnotists after much concentration. It is a naturally occurring state that we slip into and out of all the time. When we are in a trance our attention is tightly focused on our internal world and any language pattern that increases our involvement with our own internal reality will deepen the trance.

Trance plays a big part in everyday life. For example, when you are watching television you are in a sort of trance, your attention is fixed on one point and you are 'gone' from the rest of the world. People may call your name and get no response, even though your ears are working normally. On other occasions there is some external distraction and you 'snap out' of your reverie.

The traditional signs of trance to look for are: body immobility, relaxed face, slowing reflexes, time distortion, feeling distanced or dissociated. However, it need not be exactly so; for example, a computer game is a very effective trance inducer.

Day-dreaming is a form of trance, usually a very creative one. When you day-dream, you are open to ideas from your unconscious. Many scientific breakthroughs happen this way – inventors report the solution came to them in a flash as they were deeply immersed in the problem.

Everyday trances

Rather than give a more detailed description of the Milton Model, we would like to look at trance in everyday life and the practical applications that follow. Some everyday trances we have control over – we can 'snap out' of them. Others catch and hold us. Some are productive and creative – and others are negative and unresourceful. Over the page is an example of a negative trance.

Joseph was doing some consulting work for a company. His contact at the company called him and questioned the results, expressed dissatisfaction and suggested that perhaps the fee was too high. He came off the telephone and started to think about all the times when he was at school and people had questioned his work unfairly. He thought about what he had done for that company. He was sure it was good work and had dealt with the important issues. Perhaps they would not pay him! He became indignant. How dare they! It was really unfair! They had no right. He nearly marched into the next meeting ready to tell them they could keep their wretched money and he didn't want to work with the company anymore, thank you very much. This was his trance. In fact his contact had reviewed the situation and was satisfied. The cheque was in the post that day.

What are your everyday trances? Are there any unresourceful trances you repeatedly find yourself in? Find out what triggers them. It could be external, for example, a particular critical tone of voice. It could be internal, a particular thought or memory. Trance triggers are like trapdoors – once you have fallen through, it is very difficult to get back. Catch the trance before it develops and do not associate into it. If you find you are in it, then acknowledge that and come out by focusing on the external world. When you are in the present moment, you are not

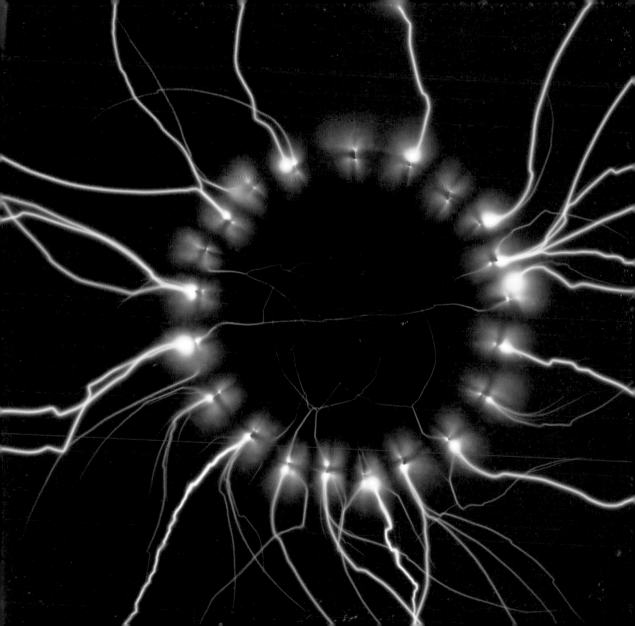

in a trance. Remember the trance is not you. It is something you go into and so it is something you can come out of.

All our trances have some purpose, they are attempts to solve problems. Think about what the trance does for you. Respect the intention and change the behaviour.

Metaphor

Metaphor is used in NLP to cover figures of speech, stories, comparisons, similes and parables. Metaphors chunk sideways from one thing to another, making comparisons and connections that may be subtle or obvious. To make sense of our experience we need to make comparisons.

Stories are our birthright and metaphors pervade our thinking. They are woven into our lives at every level, from bedtime stories we listened to as children to the ways we think about work, life, relationships and health. They build creative connections between two events or experiences, giving another different, hopefully illuminating example.

Take an example;

Life is like ...

How would you complete this and what would that mean?

Is life like a bowl of cherries? A struggle? An adventure? A school? A test? A wheel? A jungle?

The metaphors a person uses give the key to their life and the way they think. A person to whom life is an adventure is going to approach events quite differently from a person for whom life is a struggle.

Metaphors are not right or wrong, but they have consequences for how people think and act, consequences which are implicit in the metaphor.

Problem-solving

Think of a current difficult situation in your life. Think of your problem as a short metaphor. Quickly. Your problem is like ...

A jam doughnut? A ringing telephone? A poker game? A fight with a dragon?

This is your present state.

Now look at your metaphor. What are your assumptions inherent in that metaphor? What else would have to be true for that metaphor to be accurate?

Now think of what you would prefer the problem to be like. Quickly make another metaphor. You would prefer ...

Now think how the problem is like that.

What are the differences between the first metaphor and the second metaphor? How could you get from one to the other? How are they similar? The connection could be the resource that helps you from one to the other.

Giving people instructions about what they 'should' do does not work. They know already, but it is just conscious mind information. A metaphor goes beyond conscious understanding.

For example, Ian was working with a married couple who were experiencing some difficulties in their relationship. Although they basically wanted to stay together, they found it difficult to co-operate. Ian tasked them to take dancing lessons together. Both had learned to dance a little in the past, but not with each other. Dancing was a metaphor for their relationship. As they learned to dance together, they physically learned the give and take, ebb and flow, lead and follow that they had lacked in their relationship.

Beliefs and Beyond

Beliefs have us. They drive our behaviour. They are intangible and frequently unconscious. They are often confused with facts. But while a fact is what happened, a belief is a generalization about what will happen. It is a guiding principle.

We share certain beliefs about the physical world based on facts. For example, fire burns and we are subject to the laws of gravity, so we do not tempt fate by walking off cliffs or putting our hands into a fire. However, we have many beliefs about ourselves and other people that control our behaviour just as effectively as the belief that fire burns, and these may or may not be true. It is these beliefs that NLP is interested in.

When people tell you they believe something, they are either telling you of a value they hold dear or their best guess in the absence of knowledge. Beliefs answer the question 'Why?'

Belief formation

Beliefs are formed haphazardly throughout life from the meaning we give to our experience. They are formed during our upbringing from modelling significant others, especially our parents. They can be formed from a sudden unexpected conflict, trauma or confusion, and the younger we are, the more likely this is to happen. Sometimes beliefs are formed by repetition – the experience has no emotional intensity, but it just keeps happening, like water dripping on a stone.

Empowering and limiting beliefs

Some of our beliefs give us freedom, choice and open possibilities. Others may be disempowering, closing down choice. Acting as if they were true makes you and others miserable.

Beliefs are often expressed in the form:

'I can...', 'I can't...', 'I shouldn't...', 'I must...'

Take a moment to write down some examples you have of each of those four.

Do you get the sense that those that start 'I can't...' and 'I shouldn't...' limit your choices? Examine those beliefs. Ask yourself, 'What prevents me?' and 'What would happen if I did?' Even beliefs that begin 'I must...' may be problematic if you feel that this is so under all circumstances.

Belief change

Would you like to change some of your beliefs for empowering ones that make life a pleasure? The ability to choose and change your beliefs is one of the key tools NLP has to offer.

When you change a belief we suggest you replace it with another belief that keeps the positive intention of the old one. The new one must also be congruent with your sense of self.

To change a negative belief you need to ask yourself, 'What is this belief doing for me?' and 'What belief would I rather have?'

There are some good questions you can ask yourself before you consider changing any belief you have:

'How will my life be better with the new belief?'

'How might my life be worse with the new belief?'

'What is the best that could happen if I kept the old belief?'

'What is the best thing that could happen with the new belief?'

NLP has a number of techniques for changing limiting beliefs. Some work by changing the submodality structures of the old and new beliefs. Another involves going back to the imprint experience that generated the belief and re-evaluating it from a resourceful position. Whatever the technique, it is important that the new belief fits with the person's values and sense of self.

Belief and action

As already mentioned, beliefs drive behaviour. Sometimes we hold conflicting beliefs and then we will be incongruent. Sometimes people profess to believe in a particular value, but their behaviour contradicts it. Behaviour is belief in action, whatever we may consciously say we believe.

We generalize most of our beliefs, making them true or false in all contexts. Need this be so? As we have already mentioned, in NLP you can choose your beliefs. They are maps of reality. When we believe something we act as if it were true, but that does not make it true. Nor does it make it false. It will be true for you in that moment.

To understand the effect of beliefs, choose the ones you want carefully. Choose those that give you the life you wish for.

The final principle of NLP we want to address is one that makes all the others real:

If you want to understand – act.

Because the learning is in the doing. Principles make a difference in action.

For example, we hold core beliefs about our identity that have profound effects. 'I am basically a good person who makes mistakes sometimes' and 'I am a stupid person who sometimes gets it right by luck' will give very different experiences.

We also have beliefs about what lies beyond our identity. When Albert Einstein was asked what was the most important question for mankind to ask, he replied, 'The most important question facing humanity is: Is the Universe a friendly place?'

How we answer that question brings us to what it means to be a person and that takes us into the spiritual realm.

NLP and spirituality

Throughout history people have searched, driven by the feeling that there is more to life than body and mind. We are constantly reaching out beyond ourselves to know by experience our connection and unity with that which is more than ourselves. What can NLP contribute?

NLP deals with the structure of human experience and so these major issues are very relevant. Were NLP to be silent about spiritual experience, it could give the message that spiritual experience is somehow different and removed from life. This is not so. NLP itself makes no claim on reality, truth, morality or ethics. It treats them as subjective experiences. It does not acknowledge or deny an external reality, but simply suggests you act as if the presuppositions are true and notice the results you get. NLP asks not 'Is it true?' but 'Is it useful?'

How you decide what you want and how you will achieve it are ethical and moral questions. How can we use NLP in the service of ethics and aesthetics? These are necessarily the responsibility of the NLP practitioner: we each apply our own morality and ethics to both our outcomes and the means we choose to achieve them. The basis for ethics is our common humanity and deepest essence as human beings.

Spirituality could be said to be about finding our basic humanity – the essence we share with every person. One way of thinking of it is as a feeling of being most truly ourselves and in the process discovering

and becoming most deeply connected with others in their full magnificence. There are moments like this in most people's lives. You do not have to spend a lifetime of prayer and self-denial to have them. Some religious traditions hold that spiritual experiences are hard to come by, but they are all around – those splashes of joy and insight, those peak experiences when you feel most fully alive. Giving birth and becoming a parent, feeling your connection with life, looking into the eyes of a newborn child, these can all be spiritual experiences.

A universal metaphor for spiritual experience is a search, quest or journey and the end of our search, in the words of T. S. Eliot in 'The Four Quartets', will be to 'arrive where we started and know the place for the first time'. The answers on the outside are mirrored within us. Or, as Gertrude Stein put it, 'There never has been an answer, there never will be an answer – that's the answer.'

Authors

Contact Joseph O'Connor at:

c/o **Lambent Books**
4 Coombe Gardens,
New Malden,
Surrey, KT3 4AA

Tel: 020 8715 2560
Fax: 020 8715 2560
E-mail: lambent@well.com

Contact Ian McDermott at:

**International Teaching Seminars
(ITS)**
19 Widegate Street
London E1 7HP

Tel: 020 7247 0252
Fax: 020 7247 0242
www.itsnlp.com